BECOMING

A WOMAN

OF freedom

CYNTHIA HEALD

BECOMING
A *WOMAN*
OF *freedom*

NAVPRESS

NAVPRESS ◐

NavPress is the publishing ministry of The Navigators, an international Christian organization and leader in personal spiritual development. NavPress is committed to helping people grow spiritually and enjoy lives of meaning and hope through personal and group resources that are biblically rooted, culturally relevant, and highly practical.

For a free catalog go to www.NavPress.com
or call 1.800.366.7788 in the United States or 1.800.839.4769 in Canada.

© 1992, 2005 by Cynthia Heald

www.navpress.com

ISBN-13: 978-1-57683-829-7

Cover design by Disciple Design
Cover photo by Getty Images
Creative Team: Dan Rich, Steve Parolini, Darla Hightower, Arvid Wallen, Glynese Northam

Some of the anecdotal illustrations in this book are true to life and are included with the permission of the persons involved. All other illustrations are composites of real situations, and any resemblance to people living or dead is coincidental.

Unless otherwise identified, all Scripture quotations in this publication are taken from the *HOLY BIBLE: NEW INTERNATIONAL VERSION*® (NIV®). Copyright © 1973, 1978, 1984 by International Bible Society. Used by permission of Zondervan Publishing House. All rights reserved. Other versions used include: the *New American Standard Bible* (NASB), © The Lockman Foundation 1960, 1962, 1963, 1968, 1971, 1972, 1973, 1975, 1977, 1995; *The New Testament in Modern English* (PH), J. B. Phillips Translator, © J. B. Phillips 1958, 1960, 1972, used by permission of Macmillan Publishing Company; *The New English Bible* (NEB), © 1961, 1970, The Delegates of the Oxford University Press and The Syndics of the Cambridge University Press; the *Modern Language Bible: The Berkeley Version in Modern English* (MLB), copyright © 1945, 1959, 1969 by Zondervan Publishing House, used by permission; the *Williams New Testament* (WMS) by Charles B. Williams, © 1937, 1965, 1966, by Edith S. Williams, Moody Bible Institute of Chicago.

Printed in the United States of America

6 7 8 9 10 11 12 / 14 13 12 11 10 09

CONTENTS

Suggestions for Using This Study

This study is designed for both individual as well as small group use, and for women of any age or family status.

Many of the questions will guide you into Scripture passages. Ask God to reveal His truth to you through His Word, and don't be concerned about "right" or "wrong" answers. Bible study references — such as commentaries, encyclopedias, and handbooks — can help you understand particular passages by providing historical background, contexts, and common interpretations. (In a few cases, you'll need access to a standard dictionary — such as *Webster's*, *Random House*, or the *Oxford American* — for general word definitions.)

Other questions will ask you to reflect on your own life. Approach these questions honestly and thoughtfully; however, if you're doing this study in a group, don't feel that you must reveal private details of your life experiences. Use the questions under "Your Reflection" at the close of each chapter to help you work through significant issues raised by your study. If you keep a personal journal, you might want to write these reflections there rather than in this book.

You might want to memorize the key Scripture reference for each chapter, which is displayed on opening pages and listed under "Suggested Scripture Memory." You'll find that memorizing God's Word will enrich your study and deepen the significance and impact of your personal reflection.

The quotes from classic thinkers and writers have been carefully selected to enhance your understanding and enjoyment of the content in *Becoming a Woman of Freedom*. The references for these quotations (see the "Notes" section at the back of the book) will also furnish an excellent reading list for your own devotional reading and study.

PREFACE

$\mathcal{T}$he precious young woman who sat across from me at breakfast was saying, "I love God and I want to do His will, but there's something holding me back. It seems that my life is always an uphill battle. I try and try, but I get discouraged and I feel defeated."

As we spoke my heart went out to her. She really was doing all that she knew to do to grow and to serve God, but she never seemed to experience much progress, and she had no joy. She felt trapped in her Christian life, but she didn't know what to do about it. As we talked I told her that many others would say, "Yes, that is my experience, too."

Paul wrote to the Galatians, "It is for freedom that Christ has set us free. Stand firm, then, and do not let yourselves be burdened again by a yoke of slavery" (Galatians 5:1). We are in Christ, yet how easy it seems for us to be burdened by weights that enslave us and "hold us back." We have the glorious salvation of Christ, but somehow we miss out on the grace, the joy, and the freedom of the Christian life.

Hebrews 12:1-2 pictures the Christian life as a race: "Therefore, since we are surrounded by such a great cloud of witnesses, let us throw off everything that hinders and the sin that so easily entangles, and let us run with perseverance the race marked out for us. Let us fix our eyes on Jesus." As I have thought about this verse, I have realized that we all have to run our race in life. God has given us "everything we need for life and godliness" (2 Peter 1:3). What we need to do, then, is to run the race as He intended. If we "throw off everything that hinders and the sin that so easily entangles," we can begin to experience the freedom that Christ has purchased for us.

As I talked with my friend, I mentioned that I had been studying our freedom in Christ. I suggested that she might be encouraged by exploring how to lay aside the different weights and hindrances that burden us and prevent us from experiencing the freedom that the Lord longs for us to enjoy. It is the truth that sets us free, and it is the truth that we must run with in order to continue our race in freedom. As we fix our eyes on Jesus, we will have the joy and peace of running our race for His glory. And for you, my dear friend, as you are about to begin this study, I pray that you too will be helped and encouraged by the Word, by the thoughts of those who have run the race ahead of us, and by your own reflection on the race you are now running. "If the Son sets you free, you will be free indeed" (John 8:36). May God richly bless you as you become a woman of freedom.

CHAPTER ONE

Laying Aside Hindrances: *running* WITH FREEDOM

Therefore, since we are surrounded by such a great cloud of witnesses, let us throw off everything that hinders and the sin that so easily entangles, and let us run with perseverance the race marked out for us.

HEBREWS 12:1

Man's perennial efforts to take himself in hand, however he attempts it, lead to the greatest bondage in which man misses what he was meant to be. Man's true freedom does not consist of the unfettered power to direct his life, either in a political or in a Stoic sense. It lies in life with God, lived as it was originally intended by God for man. He only gains this as he denies himself. Paradoxically, the free man does not belong to himself. He belongs to him who has set him free.[1]

J. BLUNCK

*I*n literature and in Scripture, life is depicted as a race. How we choose to run the race determines our quality of life, and whom or what we choose to run toward determines our peace and joy.

All of us begin the race with a handicap—an inherited sin nature that subtly binds us and weighs us down so that the race can become strenuous and futile. God, in His great love, unbinds us, frees us from our handicap, and gives us a new nature purchased by the death of His Son.

As we admit our inadequacy to run the race alone and accept God's gracious redemption, then the race begins to have meaning, validity, and most of all, freedom. It has been observed that "none are free indeed but those whom Christ makes free."[2] We are free in Christ, but we must be aware that we often run the race with unnecessary baggage that can hinder our freedom. What is this freedom that Christ has made possible, and what can hinder us from living in freedom?

Laying Aside Hindrances

We are told in Hebrews 12 to lay aside the encumbrances, or the weights or hindrances, that keep us from running or progressing in our spiritual lives. Hannah Whitall Smith describes burdens as "everything that troubles us, whether spiritual or temporal."[3]

G. Campbell Morgan comments, "Anything which has the remotest chance of interfering with our fellowship is to put away, to be kept away."[4]

1. Look up the following words in a dictionary, and then write down a definition for each term:

   a. *Freedom*

   b. *Slavery*

c. *Hindrance*

> Every weight, that is, all inordinate affection and concern for the body, and the present life and world. Inordinate care for the present life, or fondness for it, is a dead weight upon the soul, that pulls it down when it should ascend upwards, and pulls it back when it should press forward; it makes duty and difficulties harder and heavier than they would be.[5]
>
> *Matthew Henry*

---

2. In his letter to the Romans, Paul describes the death of our old life and the gift of new life in Christ. Read Romans 6:1-14.

   a. How is our freedom accomplished?

   We die to Sin and are raised again w/ Christ

   b. What choices are now ours?

   To / not to let Sin reign in our Mortal bodies

---

3. What hindrances do you especially struggle with that keep you from experiencing freedom in Christ?

   Pride / vanity, gossip / loose tongue Judgmentalism, laziness

Running with Freedom

4. God has delivered us from the law of sin and death and from the
    tyranny of self. What does Paul teach in Romans 6:15-23 about the
    freedom God gives us and our part in experiencing that freedom?
    Write your responses in the appropriate columns.

GOD'S PART	OUR PART
- Grace - freedom from sin	- Not under the law - Obey - set free from sin - offer body in slavery to righteousness -

> Once we've tasted being alive, we can't go back to being
> dead. Aliveness in God is addictive.[6]
>
> *Nancy Groom*

Fixing Our Eyes on Jesus

Jesus exemplified freedom all of His life. He never allowed anyone or
anything to hinder His accomplishing the will of His Father. Sure of His
identity and mission, He lived, ministered, and served confidently and
securely.

5. Read Jesus' important proclamation in John 8:31-32. What do you think He means by "the truth," and in what sense does it set us free?

Jesus always did what pleased the Father. The truth is that we are given the freedom to do so through grace.

But what is the nature of our freedom? It is not release from all restraint. It is not license to indulge our sinful nature. Our freedom is the freedom to "serve one another in love." It is possible to do so, because the Holy Spirit enables us to act in ways that are contrary to the natural impulses of our sinful nature. Walking by the Spirit, we are released from the old master that produces hatred, jealousy, fits of rage, envy, and such. We are released to be loving, patient, kind, faithful and good.[7]

Lawrence O. Richards

AUTHOR'S REFLECTION—I have heard of slaves who were given freedom by the Emancipation Proclamation who still chose to live in slavery. For them, freedom was a frightening unknown. I think of the Israelites who were freed from their slavery in Egypt, yet longed for the food they received while in captivity. They were willing to become slaves again just to satisfy their appetite.

Freedom can be overwhelming, and it may seem that we are really sacrificing the "good life" to be set free by Christ. To truly understand the weight of sin and self is to begin to grasp the preciousness of our freedom in Christ. This understanding is a continuing process for me. I give up my freedom when I insist on being in control, demanding my own happiness, and building walls of protection. All of these behaviors seem right and feel comfortable, but they ultimately become heavy burdens.

God clearly calls us to "give up" this cumbersome, defeating "old self."

I think more than anything this means *grasping the truth that I have the* *power to lay aside these encumbrances.* I don't have to be a slave to sin, to myself, or to others in order to feel good about who I am. I don't have to have the world tell me what will make me happy. True freedom is realizing that apart from Christ, I am not free. If I really want to experience this "addictive aliveness," then I will throw off everything that hinders me from being truly alive. It is the only way to run.

> Most Christians are like a man who was toiling along the road, bending under a heavy burden, when a wagon overtook him and the driver kindly offered to help him on his journey. He joyfully accepted the offer but when seated in the wagon, continued to bend beneath his burden, which he still kept on his shoulders. "Why do you not lay down your burden?" asked the kind-hearted driver. "Oh!" replied the man, "I feel that it is almost too much to ask you to carry me, and I could not think of letting you carry my burden too." And so Christians, who have given themselves into the care and keeping of the Lord Jesus still continue to bend beneath the weight of their burdens, and often go weary and heavy-laden throughout the whole length of their journey.[8]
>
> *Hannah Whitall Smith*

YOUR REFLECTION — In journal form or as a prayer to the Lord, write down your thoughts in response to these two questions: *In what areas do you long to be free? How would your life be different if you were able to experience God's freedom in these areas?*

SUGGESTED SCRIPTURE MEMORY — Hebrews 12:1

CHAPTER TWO

LAYING ASIDE THE OLD SELF: *running* WITH THE NEW SELF

Strip off your old self, which follows your former ways of living and ruins you as it follows the desires that deceive you. Become new in the spirit of your minds, and put on the new self, which is created to be like God, righteous and holy in the truth.

EPHESIANS 4:22-24, MLB

It is a great grace of God to practise self-examination; but too much is as bad as too little.[1]

TERESA OF AVILA

The old self continually demands to be protected, promoted, and served. It wants to control our lives to the extent that all we do centers upon satisfying this powerful nature within us. This self cripples and burdens us.

Jesus redeemed us from the bondage of self and now gives us the power to lay it aside. How freeing not to be dominated by the old self that wants to ruin and deceive us. We must learn to consciously put off this old nature and confidently put on the new nature that is found in Christ. Recognizing our old nature and laying it aside relieves us of one of our heaviest burdens. Choosing to run with our new nature is a major step in becoming a woman of freedom.

Laying Aside the Old Self

Proverbs 16:18 states, "Pride goes before destruction, and a haughty spirit before stumbling" (NASB). Part of our old nature can manifest itself pridefully by being independent and overly self-confident.

1. Read Matthew 26:31-35, which records a conversation on the night of Christ's betrayal. How did Peter demonstrate pride?

> He placed too much confidence in himself and contradicted Jesus instead of examining his heart.

2. a. Can you recall situations in which you have responded with an attitude of "I'm sure that I would never do that"? Write down your thoughts.

> - Say stupid prideful things
> - consider myself as above someone.
> - lie about something pointless

   b. Do you think this attitude was rooted in a prideful trust in yourself? Why, or why not?

> Absolutely - I like to think I'm better off than I actually am, especially to elevate myself above someone else.

3. Another part of our old self can tell us that we're not valuable, that there's something wrong with us, that we can't do anything. A good example of this type of thinking is given in Exodus 4:10-14, which takes place during God's desert visitation to Moses in the burning bush.

   a. Read these verses and explain how Moses responded to God's command that he confront the Pharaoh and lead the Israelites out of bondage in Egypt.

   Very fearful w/ no confidence in his own ability to carry out this task

   b. Why do you think God responded the way He did to Moses (verse 14)?

   Moses should have known better than to distrust himself. God wanted him to be a vessel for his own power.

4. Does this incident in Exodus have any relevance to your own struggles with personal inadequacy? Why, or why not?

   Yes. It is not very often that I trust the Lord to do great things through my life. I only think on my own lack of ability.

Self-acceptance is basically trusting God for who I am, disabilities or physical flaws and all. We need to learn to think as George MacDonald did when he said, "I would rather be what God chose to make me than the most glorious creature that I could think of; for to have been thought about, born in God's thought, and then made by God, is the dearest, grandest, and most precious thing in all thinking."[2]

Jerry Bridges

5. Accepting ourselves is essential to being free. How would you summarize Paul's teaching in Romans 12:3-8 on the proper view of self?

I'm Really Really Really good Looking.

6. From studying the passages in questions 1 through 5, what insights are most significant to you for developing proper ways of evaluating yourself?

make Sure when I Do, I'm comparing my self to Really ugly & mean, People.

By faith we have entered into an eternal relationship with the Lord Jesus Christ. As a result, we are dead to sin and alive to God, and we now sit with Christ in the heavenlies. In Christ we *are* important, we *are* qualified, we *are* good. Satan can do absolutely nothing to alter our position in Christ and our worth to God. But he can render us virtually inoperative if he can deceive us into listening to and believing his insidious lies accusing us of being of little value to God or other people.[3]

Neil T. Anderson

Running with the New Self

Paul's frustration with his old nature causes him to lament, "Wretched man that I am! Who will set me free from the body of this death? Thanks be to God through Jesus Christ our Lord!" (Romans 7:24-25, NASB). The Lord *has* set us free: we no longer have to be trapped by an inflated ego or burdened by a frail ego.

---

7. Our identity in Christ is beautifully expressed in Ephesians 1:3-14. Study this passage and write down all that is true about us now that we have a new self.

---

8. How does this passage help you to grasp the truth that God not only accepts you, but cherishes you?

9. Receiving God's love and redemption frees us to "let go" of our old self. Read the following Scriptures and write down any insights you discover that help you experience your new life in Christ.

Luke 9:23

We must deny ourselves to experience freedom. Following Christ is freedom from self.

2 Corinthians 5:17

If we are in Christ, the old has gone away.

Galatians 2:20 *"crucified w/ Christ"*

I no longer live, Christ lives in me

> The greatest burden we have to carry in life is self. The most difficult thing we have to manage is self. . . . In laying off your burdens, therefore, the first one you must get rid of is yourself. You must hand yourself . . . into the care and keeping of your God. . . . He made you and therefore He understands you, and knows how to manage you, and you must trust Him to do it.[4]
>
> *Hannah Whitall Smith*

Fixing Our Eyes on Jesus

10. Jesus emptied Himself and took on the form of a bondservant, being made in the likeness of men (see Philippians 2:7). Read Matthew 10:39. In what sense are you losing your old life and finding a new life when you grasp the truth of your identity in Christ?

> Losing the bondage of sin
> and gaining the freedom to
> place Christ over all.

> For we would see that the one thing God wants of us is that we should empty ourselves of all our own things, in order that we may depend on Him for everything; we should discover that His purpose is to bring us to the place where we have nothing apart from Him.[5]
>
> *Henrietta Mears*

AUTHOR'S REFLECTION—My old self seems hard to lay aside. One way it manifests itself is in false humility. I will contradict someone who has sincerely complimented me. Then I will verbally put myself down, secretly hoping someone will contradict me! This is all evidence of the old self. Whether I'm taking pride in my own strength or putting myself down because of my imperfections, I'm constantly centering on my self. To be relieved of having to promote or guard my ego is truly liberating. I am the Lord's: He has created me, saved me, adopted me, and gifted me as His child. My life is His to be lived for His glory. Therefore I can graciously acknowledge any praise or any criticism (most of the time anyway!).

I so appreciate Paul's freedom from self, and his desire to finish the race well: "But I do not consider my life of any account as dear to myself, so that I may finish my course and the ministry which I received from the Lord Jesus, to testify solemnly of the gospel of the grace of God" (Acts 20:24, NASB).

YOUR REFLECTION — The manifestations of our old self appear in many forms: prideful independence, failure to recognize our worth as individuals, false comparisons of ourselves with others, preoccupation with our performance, and many others. Write out your reflections on areas in which you are especially susceptible to taking on the burdens of the old self. Then write a prayer to the Lord asking Him to help you live in the freedom of the new self in these areas.

- false comparisons of myself w/ others
- prideful independence
- Vanity (beauty and fashion)
- promoting my "intelligence"
- Speaking badly of others to make myself sound better.

SUGGESTED SCRIPTURE MEMORY: Ephesians 4:22-24

CHAPTER THREE

Laying Aside the Past: *running* with an Eternal Perspective

Therefore, if anyone is in Christ, he is a new creation; the old has gone, the new has come!
2 Corinthians 5:17

So the cross not only brings Christ's life to an end, it ends also the first life, the old life, of every one of His true followers. It destroys the old pattern, the Adam pattern, in the believer's life, and brings it to an end. Then the God who raised Christ from the dead raises the believer and a new life begins.[1]
A. W. Tozer

Our individual pasts can, to varying degrees, add internal weight to our souls. To ignore or not deal biblically with hurts, violations, and our own sin can hinder and impede our growth and progress in becoming free. The good news of the gospel is that Christ frees us from the past and gives us new life in Him. This does not mean that deep wounds and guilt automatically disappear, but it does mean that we now have freedom and power to deal righteously with our past with the Lord supporting us and guiding us along the way. How incredible that God can give us a new life that is not chained to the past, but focused on eternity.

Laying Aside the Past

1. As you begin this chapter, think about significant losses or hurts from your past that still weigh heavily on you. In what ways do these burdens keep you from feeling free to live a new life in Christ?

   My sin makes me feel trapped and barred from a relationship w/ hud.

   I have no significant losses or hurts.

2. Burdens carried from the past affect us in the present. We cannot change the past, but we must deal with it honestly in order to truly lay it aside. The Psalms give us piercing looks into agonized hearts that have been crushed by all kinds of "enemies." The psalmist's honest acknowledgment of his loss and pain can be an example for us.

   a. Psalm 142 reveals that David was deeply troubled by people who were hurting him. As you read this psalm, write down what you notice about how David dealt with his feelings before the Lord.

   He spoke very honestly and openly asked for deliverance so that he might "praise his name".

   b. In what ways does David's openness with God encourage you in acknowledging your past?

   The Lord knows every hidden thing about me. It's ok to be very real and plead w/ the Lord.

We must also come out of denial about our losses. Where formerly we had numbed our anger and pain at life's disappointments, now we must come to terms with our losses and all their accompanying emotions. . . .

Grace is freeing me to no longer minimize, justify, or deny my losses, but to face them with integrity and grieve over them. Coming out of denial about past losses has been critical to my healing process.[2]

Nancy Groom

---

3. God can free us from any burdens in our past that still hold us captive — whether sin we committed or sin that was done to us. In the following psalms, what did the psalmist discover about freedom from past burdens?

Psalm 32

The burden of unconfessed sin is overbearing. There is freedom from the guilt of sin when we confess. "Blessed is he whose transgressions are forgiven."

Psalm 116

The Lord hears our voice and is gracious and righteous, full of compassion. delivers soul from death, eyes from tears, feet from stumbling.

We are today accepted in the Beloved, absolved from sin, acquitted at the bar of God. We are even now pardoned; even now are our sins put away; even now we stand accepted in the sight of God, as though we had never been guilty. There is not a sin in the book of God, even now, against one of His people. Who dares to lay anything to their charge? There is neither speck, nor spot, nor wrinkle, nor any such thing remaining upon any one believer in the matter of justification in the sight of the Judge of all the earth.[3]

Charles H. Spurgeon

Running with an Eternal Perspective

4. As we lay aside the past, we can begin to see life from God's point of view—in light of eternity. How can the following verses help us place our past in proper perspective?

2 Corinthians 4:16-18

This world is temporary. Our struggles are pointing towards an eternal glory. We will not be struggling long.

Philippians 3:12-14

Forget what is behind and focus on the future—becoming like Christ and attaining resurrection from the dead.

Our yesterdays present irreparable things to us; it is true that we have lost opportunities which will never return, but God can transform this destructive anxiety into a constructive thoughtfulness for the future. Let the past sleep, but let it sleep on the bosom of Christ.[4]

Oswald Chambers

Fixing Our Eyes on Jesus

5. Isaiah gives us a penetrating look into Jesus' life. As we fix our eyes on Him, we realize that He was intimately acquainted with pain and rejection. Amy Carmichael writes, "The Hand that touches is the Hand that was pierced—a pierced hand is tender; it knows the feeling of pain."[5] Read Isaiah 53 and write your thoughts concerning Christ's understanding and comfort for your past hurts.

> Christ must have a tender. It is hard
> for me to believe that Jesus truly cares
> about my struggles, but then he did
> weep at Lazarus' death, knowing full well
> he was going to raise him. He wept at the
> pain of his friends.

AUTHOR'S REFLECTION—A lingering weight I carry from my past is wanting to be perfect in order to be accepted by God and other people. Whenever I fail, I tend to want to disappear from the planet. I berate myself and renew my vow never to let it happen again!

It encourages me to hear Paul say that he was not perfect and that he would not allow his past to dictate his present behavior. God certainly does not expect me to be perfect; in a sense, He is pleased when I do something right! It has been freeing to me to know that God can break destructive patterns. He can guide us into confronting the deep wounds of our past by giving us wise counselors, faithful friends, and His Spirit. He, and only He, can take away my sin and guilt.

God is in the business of freedom and newness, and it is when I acknowledge my past and confess my sin that I can begin to experience His liberty. He gives new lives for old.

I like what Nancy Groom says: "The purpose of grace is not to make us perfect but to show us our need for a Savior, then show us the Savior we need, then create in us a burning desire to be more like Him. Jesus' life in us will become evident as we open ourselves to His grace, but in this life our fallenness is interwoven with our humanness, and we'll be imperfect until we're Home."[6] Having an eternal home allows us to relinquish our past.

> You have been damaged. But you have great hope. The mercy of God does not eradicate the damage, at least not in this life, but it soothes the soul and draws it forward to a hope that purifies and sets free. Allow the pain of the past and the travail of the change process to create fresh new life in you and to serve as a bridge over which another victim may walk from death to life.[7]
>
> *Dan Allender*

YOUR REFLECTION — As you review this chapter, write down (either in journal form or as a prayer to the Lord) your feelings about your past and how you desire the Lord to guide and help you in becoming free.

Lord, teach me to continually open myself up to your grace so that you can cleanse me from sin and keep me blameless in your sight. Teach me how to be more like you and crush my desire to please my sinful nature.

SUGGESTED SCRIPTURE MEMORY: 2 Corinthians 5:17

CHAPTER FOUR

LAYING ASIDE PLEASING PEOPLE: *running* WITH FELLOWSHIP

Am I now trying to win the approval of men, or of God? Or am I trying to please men? If I were still trying to please men, I would not be a servant of Christ.

GALATIANS 1:10

Trusting in God involves the loss of our agenda, our flaming torch, so that we die to our inclination to live a lie. It requires forfeiting our rigid, self-protective, God-dishonoring ways of relating in order to embrace life as it is meant to be lived: in humble dependence on God and passionate involvement with others.[1]

DAN ALLENDER

For many of us, laying aside our bent to live for people's approval is a great burden-lifter. It is difficult to concentrate on running our race to the glory of God when we're always looking around to see if others are pleased with the way we're performing. To be bound to the capricious feelings of people is a weight that must be confronted and thrown off.

Nancy Groom calls people-pleasers "approval junkies."[2] Constantly having to seek acceptance from others leads only to further bondage, and our deep needs will not be met.

Only the Lord can fully satisfy our inner longings. Fixing our eyes on Jesus and Him alone allows us to receive His unconditional and unchanging love. His love then enables us to relate freely to others in the right way so that we can enjoy true fellowship.

We need one another's encouragement, mentoring, and love. It would be hard to run a race with no one else around to care how we were progressing! This healthy sense of mutuality springs from our complete security in Christ. As we begin to relate to people biblically, our race becomes one of great freedom and enjoyment.

Laying Aside Pleasing People

1. John 12:42-43 provides an example of people yielding to peer pressure. Why do you think they chose to respond as they did?

   They loved praise from men more than praise from God

2. How would you describe your tendencies to live for other people's approval rather than God's?

   Selfish - they are far more common than my tendencies to live for God's approval.

Approval junkies live as hostages to other people's opinions and judgments regarding their thoughts, motives, feelings, or behaviors. Approval seekers look good; they have to. . . . But people-pleasing isn't godly, nor is it healthy. Appeasers usually end up feeling used, unappreciated, and driven to become all things to all people in order to maintain their image and receive continued approval. They appear giving, but in fact they are enslaved to their insatiable need to be admired.[3]

Nancy Groom

---

3. No one could accuse Paul of being an approval seeker! His passion was to please God. Study 1 Thessalonians 2:1-12. Describe the ways in which Paul related to the Thessalonians in freedom rather than from a need for their approval.

He related to them as a father would to a child, seeing the ways they needed to grow and preaching despite strong opposition. They never used flattery or pretended to be something else.

4. Paul wrote, "I am a free man and own no master; but I have made myself every man's servant, to win over as many as possible" (1 Corinthians 9:19, NEB). What does 1 Corinthians 2:1-5 reveal about why Paul was free to be vulnerable and intimately involved in other people's lives?

He put aside any feelings of superiority and spoke very simply so there would be no question as to his intent.
They were not pointed towards Paul as a great leader and preacher but to God's power.

5. If you were able to replace your approval-seeking tendencies with Paul's relational freedom, how would your life be different?

I would spend less money, I would annoy lots more people, no one would feel put down by me.

> Our union with Jesus is the basis for a bond with our
> fellow Christians. Because that bond is so vital and real,
> we can live with each other in an intimacy impossible
> in every other setting.[4]
>
> *Lawrence O. Richards*

Running with Fellowship

Our completeness in Christ enables us to be an integral part of the body of believers so that we can exhort, encourage, and serve one another. We do not withdraw from people because Christ is our sufficiency; rather, His sufficiency thrusts us out in confidence to risk intimacy with others.

6. What do the following passages teach about how we are to participate in this vital fellowship of believers?

John 13:34-35

We love one another, meaning we put their needs above our own, do not compete and act selflessly.

1 Thessalonians 5:14-15

Hold others accountable, encourage timid, be patient w/ everyone and kind.

Hebrews 10:23-25

Encourage each other to press on and do good

Please his neighbour, not in every thing, it is not an unlimited rule; but *for his good*, especially for the good of his soul: not to please him by serving his wicked wills, and humouring him in a sinful way, or consenting to his enticements, or suffering sin upon him; this is a base way of pleasing our neighbour to the ruin of his soul: if we thus please men, we are not the servants of Christ; but please him for his good; not for our own secular good, or to make a prey of him, but for his spiritual good. To edification, that is, not only for his profit, but for the profit of others, to edify the body of Christ, by studying to oblige one another.[5]

Matthew Henry

---

7. What do you think are your strongest and your weakest areas of fellowship with other believers?

Strongest
compassion
openness
Humor

Weakest
competition
standoffishness
abrasiveness (being forceful)

Fixing Our Eyes on Jesus

8. Jesus said, "He who sent Me is with Me; He has not left Me alone, for I always do the things that are pleasing to Him" (John 8:29, NASB). The Lord deeply loved and ministered to people, but He never compromised the truth or His mission because of what people might think. Read these Scriptures and describe how Jesus related to the Pharisees and to the multitude.

   Matthew 9:9-13

   Mark 1:35-38

9. How can you follow Jesus' example in your relationships with people?

Our Lord . . . was never suspicious, never bitter, never in despair about any man, because He put God first in trust; He trusted absolutely in what God's grace could do for any man. If I put my trust in human beings first, I will end in despairing of everyone; I will become bitter, because I have insisted on man being what no man can ever be — absolutely right. Never trust anything but the grace of God in yourself or in anyone else.[6]

Oswald Chambers

AUTHOR'S REFLECTION — Several years ago I spoke at a seminar and I happened to read some of the evaluations. Some of the comments about me were not all that favorable — I was not entertaining; I was too serious. And because I am such a people-pleaser, I was also devastated! I went to the Lord and said, "That's it, Lord, I'm taking a vow of silence; I will never speak in public again."

Over the next few days, God very gently began to speak to my heart. This is what I heard: "Apparently, all that concerns you is whether people like you or not. Does what I think matter to you? If I am pleased with what you do, is that enough? If I want you to speak, and no one responds, will you speak for just Me?"

It has not been easy to lay aside my people-pleasing. I'm still in the process, but I'm beginning to experience the incredible freedom of letting go of that weight in my life. As I draw on the Lord's unfathomable love for me and fix my heart on pleasing only Him, then I find that I can give myself to others in ways that I never could before when I was intent on their approval. I need to be sensitive and open to others' opinions, but I no longer become paralyzed because I haven't pleased everyone.

I can now speak the truth in love and with confidence. I can fellowship and serve in freedom. I can also be vulnerable and accountable to others because I'm not always jockeying for position or doing things for their acceptance. I really do appreciate and cherish positive feedback from people, but I no longer have to have it to run my race.

YOUR REFLECTION — Take a few minutes to reflect in prayer about your need for dependence on God, your approval-seeking patterns, and your desire for biblical involvement with others. Write down how you feel the Lord is speaking to you, or how you desire Him to free you for greater security in Christ and true fellowship with people.

SUGGESTED SCRIPTURE MEMORY: Galatians 1:10

CHAPTER FIVE

Laying Aside Bitterness: *running* with Forgiveness

You must remove all bitterness, rage, anger, threats, and insults, with all malice. You must practice being kind to one another, tender-hearted, forgiving one another, just as God through Christ has graciously forgiven you.

Ephesians 4:31-32, wms

We have cause to suspect our religion if it does not make us gentle, and forbearing, and forgiving; if the love of our Lord does not so flood our hearts as to cleanse them of all bitterness, and spite, and wrath. If a man is nursing anger, if he is letting his mind become a nest of foul passions, malice, hatred, and evil wishing, how dwelleth the love of God in him?[1]

Hugh Black

*H*ow direct and specific the Word of God is concerning our removing, putting away, and laying aside all bitterness, wrath, and anger.

These emotions betray deep, abiding weights that cling to us and continually hinder us from running our race in freedom.

The bitterness and anger we need to confront in this chapter is the kind we nurse: it has "put down roots" and dwells within us to intrude and disrupt at will. *Orge*, the Greek word for anger, "suggests a more settled or abiding condition of mind, frequently with a view to taking revenge."[2] *Pikria*, the Greek word for bitterness, means "to cut, to prick, hence, lit., pointed, sharp, keen, pungent to the sense of taste, smell, etc."[3] Have you ever run and felt a sharp prick in your side? That's what it's like to live daily with bitterness. No wonder we are told to "remove it"!

Laying Aside Bitterness

1. The roots of bitterness often remain buried, only occasionally surfacing to prick our awareness with painful memories. What experiences in your life have you been aware of that carry the sting of bitterness?

   Ex-boyfriends
   things Said about me.

2. Synonyms for bitterness include: "harshness, resentment, grudge, animosity, hostility, indignation, anger, venom, spitefulness, maliciousness, sarcasm, testiness, viciousness, malice."[4] What disagreeable words! God's Word does address these emotions. What counsel does Paul give in Ephesians 4:25-32 concerning anger and bitterness?

   Do not sin in anger, only let
   wholesome Speech come from your mouth.
   Anger grieves the spirit.

3. The writer of Hebrews spoke specifically of a root of bitterness. In order to understand the context of this verse, it is necessary to read Hebrews 12:1-17. After carefully reading this passage, write down your thoughts to these questions.

   a. In what way are we to run the race (verse 1)?

   Throwing off everything that entangles

   b. How is Jesus an example for us (verses 2-4)?

   Endured the same for the joy set before him

   c. How are we to view God's discipline (verses 5-13)?

   As sons. It is a loving action

   d. What is the goal of God's training (verses 10-13)?

   To make us holy and righteous

   e. Why are we to pursue peace and sanctification (verses 14-17)?

   So we don't miss the grace of God and can see the Lord.

   f. Why do you think the writer included a warning about bitterness (verse 15) in this context?

   It's a root, meaning it grows to cause trouble and defile many.

Bitterness in the NT focuses on that angry and resent-
ful state of mind that can develop when we undergo
troubles. . . . The writer [of Hebrews] describes the
hardships that come into our lives and speaks of them
as God's discipline. They are a form of training that
God in love has determined we need for our own good.
Crushing experiences never seem pleasant at the time.
They are painful. It is only later that we see their fruit
in inner peace and righteousness. But an experience
intended for our good can be twisted into bitterness.
The writer points out that to profit as God intends, we
must not surrender to hopelessness. We must struggle,
in God's holy way, to live at peace with all around us and
not give way to bitterness. . . . The remedy for bitterness,
then, is the appropriation of God's grace.[5]

Lawrence O. Richards

---

4. Jeremiah vividly described his (and the Israelites') bitterness in
   Lamentations 3. Read the following verses in this chapter and com-
   ment on how Jeremiah handled his feelings of bitterness.

   Verses 5,15,19-20

   He will remember the affliction
   and bitterness

   Verses 21-26

   He will wait for God.
   His hope is in his love.

Verses 39-40

*He is only being punished
for sins. Needs to examine himself.*

Verses 57-59

*God sees the wrong done
and will uphold.*

---

5. Bitterness is intensely personal, as the writer of Proverbs confirmed: "Each heart knows its own bitterness" (14:10). Have you in any way tended to ignore your own roots of bitterness, hoping that they would go away if left alone or fearing that resolving them would be too difficult? If so, write down your thoughts about what kinds of effects these untended roots have had in your life.

Yes.

Bitterness arises in our hearts when we do not trust in the sovereign rule of God in our lives. If ever anyone had a reason to be bitter it was Joseph. Sold by his jealous brothers into slavery, falsely accused by his master's immoral wife, and forgotten by one he had helped in prison, Joseph never lost sight of the fact that God was in control of all that happened to him. In the end he was able to say to his brothers, "You meant evil against me, but God meant it for good in order to bring about this present result, to preserve many people alive" (Genesis 50:20).[6]

Jerry Bridges

Running with Forgiveness

6. To keep from being bitter toward hurtful people in our lives, we must personally realize that the grace of God enables us to forgive as we have been forgiven. What do the following passages teach about forgiveness?

Ephesians 1:7-8

God lavishes us w/ forgiveness and grace.

1 John 1:9

Confess bitterness and God will cleanse and forgive.

Forgiveness is the divine miracle of grace; it cost God the Cross of Jesus Christ before He could forgive sin and remain a holy God. . . . Sanctification is simply the marvellous expression of the forgiveness of sins in a human life, but the thing that awakens the deepest well of gratitude in a human being is that God has forgiven sin. Paul never got away from this. When once you realize all that it cost God to forgive you, you will be held as in a vise, constrained by the love of God.[7]

Oswald Chambers

7. Our forgiveness is a divine miracle! With this forgiveness, however, comes the responsibility to extend it to others. Forgiveness means "to let go, cancel, release, pardon." What does Jesus' parable in Matthew 18:21-35 teach about releasing others?

Forgive eternally - never stop

8. How does Paul's exhortation in Colossians 3:12-13 support Jesus' teaching in the parable of the unmerciful servant?

*Forgive whatever grievances.
Have no self inflected awareness*

You don't forgive someone merely for their sake; you do it for your sake so you can be free. Your need to forgive isn't an issue between you and the offender; it's between you and God. Forgiveness is agreeing to live with the consequences of another person's sin. Forgiveness is costly; we pay the price of the evil we forgive. Yet you're going to live with those consequences whether you want to or not; your only choice is whether you will do so in the bitterness of unforgiveness or the freedom of forgiveness. . . . Forgiveness deals with your pain, not another's behavior.[8]

Neil T. Anderson

Fixing Our Eyes on Jesus

The Lord beautifully exemplifies grace and forgiveness. He taught so forcefully on forgiveness because it is so vital to our freedom. Charles Swindoll writes, "[Jesus] said that we who refuse to forgive—we who live in the gall of bitterness—will become victims of torture, meaning intense inner torment.... For your sake, let me urge you to 'put away all bitterness' now.... The escape route is clearly marked. It leads to the cross ... where the only One who had a right to be bitter wasn't."[9]

---

9. What can you discover from Jesus' example in dealing with bitterness toward people who have hurt you? See Luke 23:32-34.

> No bitterness -
> They don't know what they do -
> Compassion for others who are bitter
> and wrong you.

AUTHOR'S REFLECTION—Bitterness and anger are indeed heavy weights. It is in responding to our pain, though, that we learn endurance and realize that all of this is the process of sanctification—becoming like Jesus. It has been important for me in learning to forgive to first acknowledge my hurt and my feelings to the Lord—just as Jeremiah did. I find it helpful to write my feelings down to fully express my emotions.

One of my favorite passages is Psalm 55. In this psalm, David tells of being forsaken by a close friend. He is devastated, but writes, "As for me, I shall call upon God, and the LORD will save me. Evening and morning and at noon, I will complain and murmur, and He will hear my voice" (verses 16-17, NASB). He ends by encouraging all: "Cast your burden upon the LORD, and He will sustain you" (verse 22, NASB).

Where else can we go any time of the day or night when we're hurting? Oswald Chambers observes, "Prayer is the exercise of drawing on the grace of God."[10] It is only as I draw on His grace that I can forgive—confident that it is for my good and that I am doing what God has asked me to do: to love. Bitterness enslaves us, but forgiveness frees us as nothing else. No runner should be without it.

YOUR REFLECTION — Take time to consider prayerfully what the Lord might be saying to you about dealing with bitterness in your life. Write down your thoughts.

SUGGESTED SCRIPTURE MEMORY: Ephesians 4:31-32

CHAPTER SIX

Laying Aside Busyness: *running* WITH REST

Because I called, but no one answered; I spoke, but they did not listen. And they did evil in My sight and chose that in which I did not delight.

Isaiah 66:4, nasb

Only through a relationship with the Lord can we experience the blessing of the rest that God has for those who trust him.[1]

Lawrence O. Richards

Someone once said that many of us are so busy that if God wanted to speak to us, He'd have to leave a message on our answering machine!

Being overly busy is one of the reasons I began to study our freedom in Christ. I became aware that the frenzied race I was in was probably not the race or the pace that the Lord had planned for me. Charles Swindoll says that "God wants our lifestyle to be easier than most of us realize."[2] Our comprehension of what it is to serve Him gets blurred in our zeal and in our old sin nature.

Most of us today run in the fast lane of life. We choose this "lane" for a myriad of reasons. We must examine the bulky weight of constant busyness, for we will have difficulty finishing our race at the speed with which some of us are running. If we're going to persevere, then we must learn to *run* with *rest*, the comfort and refreshment that the Lord so lovingly provides.

Laying Aside Busyness

1. As you run your daily race, what are the red flags that let you know when you're too busy?

2. What guidelines did Paul give in Colossians 1:9-12 for living sensibly in dependence upon the Lord?

> Don't be unwise enough to think that we are serving God best by constant activity at the cost of headaches and broken rest. I am getting to be of the opinion that we may be doing too much. We want—at least this is my own want—a higher quality of work. Our labor should be to maintain unbroken communion with our blessed Lord; then we shall have entire rest, and God abiding in us; that which we do will not be ours, but His.[3]
>
> *John Kenneth MacKenzie*

3. God pays close attention to what we do with our time and abilities. Read 1 Corinthians 3:10-13, and reflect on how your busyness could be characterized as "wood, hay, and straw" rather than the lasting value of "gold, silver, and costly stones." In what ways does your busyness keep you from living the way you would really like to live?

4. Think about *why* you stay busy. Check any of the following possible reasons that apply to you. (You may want to add your own ideas to the list.)

❏   I have too many demands on my life.

❏   I like to feel needed.

❏   I like the approval I get from others.

❏   It's hard for me to say no.

❏   I feel guilty if I'm not busy.

❏   If I stay busy, I don't have to face the difficult areas of my life.

❏   Staying busy relieves me of the need to make decisions about how I spend my time.

❏   Busyness gives me a sense of control over my life.

❏   Other:

When we stop to evaluate, we realize that our dilemma goes deeper than shortage of time; it is basically the problem of priorities. . . . We sense uneasily that we may have failed to do the important. The winds of other people's demands have driven us onto a reef of frustration. We confess, quite apart from our sins, "We have left undone those things which we ought to have done; and we have done those things which we ought not to have done."[4]

Charles E. Hummel

Running with Rest

If we're running, how can we be resting at the same time? Physical rest is very important, but in order to keep running we also need an *inner* rest — the peace and refreshment that come only from the Lord. Oswald Chambers describes this inner rest: "I will stay you. Not — I will put you to bed and hold your hand and sing you to sleep; but — I will get you out of bed, out of the languor and exhaustion, out of the state of being half dead while you are alive; I will imbue you with the spirit of life, and you will be stayed by the perfection of vital activity."[5]

God's rest can be ours. It comes as we abide in Him and stay active in *His business*, not our busyness.

---

5. Read the following passages, and then choose one that speaks most strongly to your desire for freedom from busyness. Write down your thoughts about how this word from the Lord can help you to experience the true rest He offers.

Psalm 23:1-3; Ecclesiastes 4:6; Isaiah 30:15-16; Jeremiah 6:16; Matthew 11:28-30

What is "resting in God," but the instinctive movement and upward glance of the spirit to him; the confiding all one's griefs and fears to him, and feeling strengthened, patient, hopeful in the act of doing so! It implies a willingness that he should choose for us, a conviction that the ordering of all that concerns us is safer in his hands than in our own.[6]

James D. Burns

---

6. It has been wisely noted, "We cannot make up for failure in our devotional life by redoubling energy in service."[7] The two sisters, Mary and Martha, give vivid pictures of "rest" and "busyness." The Lord was in their home and observed the choices each of them made to serve Him. Read Luke 10:38-42.

   a. How did Jesus respond to each of the sisters?

   b. What do you think Jesus meant when He said that Mary had chosen the "good part" or what was "better"?

The times I've overworked and made myself and everyone else miserable, it's been because I needed people's
appreciation, or their pity, or their admiration too
much. I was trying to prove I was worth something by
my hard work. . . . But when service becomes a pain, or
a means of personal gain, then the service needs to be
curtailed for the sake of the higher good of resting in
Christ's presence. God called you to be His beloved, not
His beast of burden.[8]

Frank Barker

Fixing Our Eyes on Jesus

7. Someone has observed that Jesus was never in a hurry. His life empha-
    sizes the importance of taking time to be with our Father. As you
    read Luke 5:15-16, write down your thoughts about the importance
    of withdrawing in order to rest from busyness.

AUTHOR'S REFLECTION—As I have examined my schedule, I've found
that I tend to "busy" myself so that I can avoid doing some of the important things in my life that take discipline. The activities or responsibilities
that I tend to "put off" range from writing letters to doing major projects.
If I'm busy doing "good" things, then I have an adequate excuse for not
doing the other important things.

I remember committing myself to a project that would take a lot of
time and effort. In the midst of that commitment, though, I found myself
choosing to be involved in all kinds of other activities. It was then I real-

ized that I was doing these other things really to evade working on the project. This same tendency carries over into my choosing to have time with the Lord. I want to spend time with Him, but it takes discipline to withdraw from all the good things that demand my attention.

I think this is why Jesus commended Mary's choice to sit at His feet. Like Martha, we can allow constant busyness to crowd out the gold, silver, and precious stones in our lives. Chambers writes, "The main thing about Christianity is not the work we do, but the relationship we maintain and the atmosphere produced by that relationship. That is all God asks us to look after, and it is the one thing that is being continually assailed."[9]

To pace ourselves in our race, we must make it a priority to withdraw to replenish ourselves spiritually, emotionally, and physically. We cannot allow ourselves to let busyness control our lives, so that we fall down exhausted at the end of the race. That is not freedom! There is much to do in this life, but God wants us to do all that we do in His Name and to His glory. To honor that request, we must come to Him often for the inner rest, refreshment, and guidance that is needed to run our race.

YOUR REFLECTION — Reflect on your desire for rest in the Lord, and on the busyness that pulls you down in running with freedom. Write down your thoughts about what demands or activities in your life you want to leave behind as unnecessary weights, and where you might be able to create opportunities for "inner rest."

SUGGESTED SCRIPTURE MEMORY: Isaiah 66:4

CHAPTER SEVEN

Laying Aside Anxiety:
running
WITH PEACE

Be anxious for nothing, but in everything by prayer and supplication with thanksgiving let your requests be made known to God. And the peace of God, which surpasses all comprehension, will guard your hearts and your minds in Christ Jesus.

PHILIPPIANS 4:6-7, NASB

Areas of legitimate anxiety exist even for the strongest of believers. But the pressures of even legitimate concerns are not to dominate us or to make us habitually anxious, worried people. We escape by using anxiety creatively. This means that we must recognize the feelings of pressure and concern as a call to prayer. We should immediately turn to God to lay our needs and the needs of others before him. We then turn back to live our lives encompassed by his peace. Anxiety, rather than drawing us away from God, draws us to him and thus fulfills his purpose for it in our lives.[1]

LAWRENCE O. RICHARDS

*A*n anxious person is "distressed, disturbed, worried, troubled, concerned, uneasy, ill at ease, disquieted, restless, nervous"![2] Sounds like anxiety is certainly something that needs to be laid aside! The freedom that Christ gives includes freedom from the control of all of the above. To live distressed and worried lives hinders us in every way and keeps us from running well.

The rest and peace of Christ are real, and He longs for us to possess them in their fullest measure. He is always available when a concern arises, and He cares about our cares. Our part is to avail ourselves of His strength and peace. It's not easy to lay aside anxiety, but it is necessary if we want to run freely.

Laying Aside Anxiety

1. Scripture is anything but vague when it comes to instructing us about anxiety and worry. It's comforting, in a way, to know that the Lord understands that we will have anxiety. Read these verses and record their encouragements.

    Isaiah 35:3-4

    - Strengthen feeble hands
    - Steady knees that give way
    - God will come to save

    Isaiah 41:10

    - I am w/ you
    - I am your God
    - I will strengthen you and help you
    - I will uphold you

Fretting springs from a determination to get our own way. Our Lord never worried and He was never anxious, because He was not "out" to realize His own ideas; he was "out" to realize God's ideas. . . . Deliberately tell God that you will not fret about that thing. All our fret and worry is caused by calculating without God.[3]

Oswald Chambers

---

2. a. In the Sermon on the Mount Jesus addresses the burden of worry. Read Matthew 6:25-34 and write down the Lord's teaching on anxiety.

God Knows all of our needs. He provides
food and clothing for the flowers and
birds; how much more will he provide for me?

b. What does this passage tell us about God's care and provision for our needs?

Just Seek first his Kingdom and
righteousness. God will take
care of everything else.

Both anxiety and worry spring from natural and legitimate concerns that are part of life in this world. But legitimate concerns are handled wrongly when they do one or more of the following: (1) become dominating concerns in our life and lead to fear, (2) destroy our perspective on life and cause us to forget that God exists and cares, or (3) move us to drift into an attitude of constant worry and concern over a future that we cannot control.[4]

Lawrence O. Richards

3. Read Psalm 55:22 and 1 Peter 5:6-7. Describe what you think it means to "cast" our anxieties on the Lord.

Give them completely to God.
Throw off the weight of the burden and
leave it to God to take care of.

> Because God cares for you, you can cast your anxiety on Him. Do not get these thoughts reversed. The text does not say, "If you cast your anxieties on Him, He will care for you." His care is not conditioned on our faith and our ability to cast our anxiety on Him; rather, it is because He does care for us that we can cast our anxiety on Him.[5]
>
> *Jerry Bridges*

Running with Peace

4. Jesus gives us His peace (see John 14:27). We can appropriate His peace in several ways. As you read these verses, identify the source of the writer's comfort and tranquility.

Psalm 94:19

God's consolation

Psalm 119:165

Love for God's law

Isaiah 26:3

A steadfast mind who trusts in God.

---

5. Are you able to appropriate these same sources of comfort and peace? Explain.

Sometimes. My mind is not always steadfast, and my faith wavers. But I do derive a great deal of comfort from the Lord.

---

6. Prayer enables us to receive God's peace. Study Philippians 4:6-7 and write down what you learn about how we are to pray, and the results that can be ours.

Present every request, along w/ thanksgiving

The result is peace and a knowledge that God is faithful.

> Thanksgiving gives effect to prayer and frees from anxious carefulness by making all God's dealings a matter for praise, not merely for resignation, much less murmuring. Peace is the companion of thanksgiving.[6]

7. It seems that King David continually dealt with anxiety. Three of his prayers are listed below. What can you learn from these prayers that will help you to receive God's peace?

Psalm 38:18

Confess your sins

Psalm 62:5-8

God alone is our rock and salvation. Faith

Psalm 139:23-24

Ask God to search you and lead you, and show you offensive ways.

When I am tossed to and fro with various reasonings, distractions, questionings, and forebodings, I will fly to my true rest. From my sinful thoughts, my vain thoughts, my sorrowful thoughts, my griefs, my cares, my conflicts, I will hasten to the Lord; he has divine comforts, and these will not only console but actually delight me. How sweet are the comforts of the Spirit! Who can muse upon eternal love, immutable purposes, covenant promises, finished redemption, the risen Saviour, his union with his people, the coming glory, and such like themes without feeling his heart leaping with joy? The little world within us, like the great world without, is full of confusion and stife; but when Jesus enters it, and whispers "Peace be unto you," there is a calm, yea, a rapture of bliss.[7]

Charles H. Spurgeon

Fixing Our Eyes on Jesus

8. A. W. Tozer has commented that Jesus died as calmly as He lived. Based on John 16:32-33, what can you learn about peace from Jesus' teaching on the night of His betrayal?

He has already overcome the world.

> Let us but feel that He has His heart set upon us, that He is watching us from those heavens with tender interest, that He is following us day by day as a mother follows her babe in his first attempt to walk alone, that He has set His love upon us, and in spite of ourselves is working out for us His highest will and blessing, as far as we will let Him — and then nothing can discourage us.[8]
>
> *A. B. Simpson*

AUTHOR'S REFLECTION — Recently, I was quite anxious about a particular, painful circumstance in my life. I was in much prayer — asking for God's will and letting my requests continually come before Him. I prayed as I had never prayed before, but I remained anxious; I was not experiencing the peace of God.

As I meditated on Philippians 4:6-7 (wondering why it wasn't working!), I realized that I was doing everything Paul said to do except to pray with thanksgiving. To be honest, I couldn't think of anything I could really be thankful for in this situation. But Paul says to pray and ask with thanksgiving — then the peace of God will follow.

As I began to pray with thankfulness — thanking God for His hearing my requests, His great love, concern, and understanding of my hurt, His sovereignty, His power to redeem — then, and only then, did I begin to know the peace of God which transcends all understanding. My circumstances didn't change, and I still didn't know how things would work out, but I was no longer "tied up" inside. I was free to trust.

God has made it very clear in His Word that He does not want us to lead anxious lives. He doesn't want us to run our race while burdened down with worry; in fact, He tells us that if we have a burden, we should cast it on Him. How unwise of us not to take Him up on His offer! He wants us to run freely in peace. That's why He came, and that's why He lives within us. "Praise be to the Lord, to God our Savior, who daily bears our burdens" (Psalm 68:19).

YOUR REFLECTION—As a way of presenting your anxieties to the Lord, write them down in simple list form and then tell God about them in prayer. Record any thoughts or reflections concerning how you can receive God's peace.

SUGGESTED SCRIPTURE MEMORY: Philippians 4:6-7

Laying Aside Doubt and Fear:
running
WITH FAITH AND TRUST

"Do not tremble, do not be afraid. Did I not proclaim this and foretell it long ago? You are my witnesses. Is there any God besides me? No, there is no other Rock; I know not one."

ISAIAH 44:8

God's unfailing love for us is an objective fact affirmed over and over in the Scriptures. It is true whether we believe it or not. Our doubts do not destroy God's love, nor does our faith create it. It originates in the very nature of God, who is love, and it flows to us through our union with His beloved Son.[1]

JERRY BRIDGES

At one point in his ministry the apostle Paul wrote, "For when we came into Macedonia, this body of ours had no rest, but we were harassed at every turn—conflicts on the outside, fears within"

(2 Corinthians 7:5). Can you identify? This race we are in has numerous opportunities for doubt and fear. If we don't run with faith and trust, our race has no joy, no peace, and certainly no freedom. Many have gone before us, though, who were able to run victoriously despite their wavering. As we study their lives, we see that the Source of their strong faith and trust can be ours as well.

Laying Aside Doubt and Fear

1. Using a dictionary, write out definitions for the words *doubt* and *fear*.

   a. *Doubt*

   b. *Fear*

2. Read all of Psalm 73.

   a. What were the psalmist's doubts and fears?

   He doubted whether his righteous life was worth it. The wicked were flourishing and free from burden.

   b. How did the psalmist work through his struggles?

   He reminds himself that they will all perish and God is all he has.

3. What kinds of doubts and fears interfere most often with your ability to trust God?

> Infallibility of the Bible
> Eternality of Salvation
> Gift of tongues
> Whether God is real

Those who trust God most are those whose faith permits them to risk wrestling with Him over the deepest questions of life. Good hearts are captured in a divine wrestling match; fearful, doubting hearts stay clear of the mat. The commitment to wrestle will be honored by a God who will not only break but bless. Jacob's commitment to wrestle with God resulted in the wounding of his thigh. He would never again walk without a limp. But the freedom in his heart was worth the price of his shattered limb.[2]

Dan Allender

4. David's faith was tested many times, but in those times of testing he always went to the Lord. Psalm 27 exemplifies David's confidence in God despite his fears. Read this psalm out loud, and then write down any insights you discover in it that are relevant to the doubts and fears you identified in question 3.

> vs. 8,9 — Do not hide your face from me
> ✗ These verses do not really relate
> to my doubts.

5. What do the following passages teach us about why we can be free from fear?

Romans 8:14-17

We do not have a spirit of fear but a spirit of sonship.

Hebrews 2:14-15

God has destroyed the devil (who held the power of death)

1 John 4:15-19

There is no fear in love. We do not have to fear punishment.

When once you are rooted in Reality, nothing can shake you. If your faith is in experiences, anything that happens is likely to upset that faith; but nothing can ever upset God or the almighty Reality of Redemption; base your faith on that, and you are as eternally secure as God.[3]

Oswald Chambers

Running with Faith and Trust

6. The letter to the Hebrews devotes an entire chapter to recounting the lives of those who persevered in faith. These are the witnesses who surround us like a cloud while we run our race (see Hebrews 12:1). These role models from the history of God's people both define and exemplify faith in action. Read Hebrews 11 and write down your understanding of what faith is.

Being sure of what we hope for and certain of what we do not see.

> The people of God are tough. For long centuries those who belong to the world have waged war against the way of faith, and they have yet to win. . . . The way of faith is not a fad that is taken up in one century only to be discarded in the next. It lasts. It is a way that works. It has been tested thoroughly.[4]
>
> *Eugene H. Peterson*

7. Sometimes the idea of placing our faith and trust in God can seem too difficult for us, especially when we're caught in the grip of doubt and fear. What do the following passages teach about the source of faith?

Ephesians 2:8-9

It is the gift of God.

Hebrews 12:2

Jesus authors and perfects our faith

There are two places of advantage into which deserting souls may retire: the name of God, and the absolute promises of the gospel. I think of these as the fair havens, which are chiefly of use when the storm is so great that the ship cannot live at sea. As there was nothing inherent in the creature to move the great God to make such promises, so there can be nothing in the creature to hinder the Almighty from keeping them, where and when He pleases. This act of faith in retreating to the promises, accompanied with a longing desire after that grace you are seeking, while it may not fully satisfy all your doubts, will nevertheless keep you from sinking.[5]

William Gurnall

Fixing Our Eyes on Jesus

8. Jesus not only spoke often on the importance of faith, He was wholly faithful and trustworthy. He continually sought to teach His disciples the security they had in Him.

   a. Read the event recorded in Matthew 8:23-27. What is the lesson Jesus wanted His disciples to learn?

   > Fear arises out of the absence of faith

   b. Do you trust God to calm the storms in your life? Why, or why not?

   > The big ones, yes, H the little everyday nagging doubts I can't shake.

AUTHOR'S REFLECTION—After Paul acknowledged his fears to the Corinthians, in the very next sentence he wrote, "But God . . ." (2 Corinthians 7:6). When we are overwhelmed with apprehension, we must learn the "But God" response. "But God" sent Titus to encourage Paul. "But God" revealed Himself to Asaph in the sanctuary. "But God" was David's light and salvation. "But God" calmed the storm for the fearful disciples. "But God," when we turn to Him whether plagued by doubt or by fear, is our Rock: There is no other.

Whenever we begin to doubt, we must not waver in our faith, but be fully assured that what God has promised, He is also able to perform (see Romans 4:21). God has pledged Himself to be our defense, our refuge, our strength, and "He has granted to us His precious and magnificent promises" (2 Peter 1:4, NASB). He is our hiding place when we are fearful, and He is our confidence when we are doubtful. Our trust in His love and strength are indispensable to staying on course in the race that is set before us.

YOUR REFLECTION—What have you discovered in this lesson that could help you develop a "But God" mindset in response to your doubts and fears?

Faith does not originate in myself.

SUGGESTED SCRIPTURE MEMORY: Isaiah 44:8

CHAPTER NINE

LAYING ASIDE THE FLESH: *running* WITH THE SPIRIT

I run the race then with determination. I am no shadow-boxer, I really fight! I am my body's sternest master, for fear that when I have preached to others I should myself be disqualified.

1 CORINTHIANS 9:26-27, PH

I know this, that the death of all that is sinful in me is my soul's highest ambition, yes, and the death of all that is carnal. And all that savors of the old Adam. Oh, that it would die. And where can it die but at the feet of Him who has the new life, and who by manifesting Himself in all His glory is to purge away our dross and sin?[1]

CHARLES H. SPURGEON

Our old, sinful nature, when in control of our lives, is at enmity with the freedom of our new nature in Christ. Our flesh needs buffeting and laying aside, so that we do not cling to sin. Paul writes that "the mind set on the flesh is death . . . is hostile toward God . . . and those who are in the flesh cannot please God" (Romans 8:6-8, NASB). We are told in Hebrews 12:1 to throw off the sin that entangles us. We certainly can't run if our feet are enmeshed!

We must be uncompromising in dealing with the lusts of the flesh and sin in our lives if we are to run the race in freedom and to the glory of God. Jesus said very simply, "It is the Spirit who gives life; the flesh profits nothing" (John 6:63, NASB).

Laying Aside the Flesh

1. What is this "flesh" that we are to lay aside? Galatians 5:16-21 describes the deeds of the flesh and gives us insight into our old nature. Write down the characteristics of our sinful disposition.

   Sexual immorality, impurity, debauchery, Idolatry, witchcraft, hatred, discord, Jealousy, rage, selfish ambition, dissensions, factions, envy, drunkenness and orgies

2. With great insight into our human frailty, Paul pictures our struggle with indwelling sin in Romans 7. Although we are in Christ, we still have to contend with our flesh. Study Romans 7:14-25 and summarize Paul's description of the conflict between the law of sin and God's law.

   We have two natures at war with each other in our body. The sin nature often controls us and we sin naturally, though we don't even want it.

   Why do we entertain tempting thoughts which are contrary to God's Word and God's will? Let's face it—we do so because we want to. We're not tempted by foods we don't like, by unattractive members of the opposite sex, by unwanted promotions, etc. Temptation's hook is the devil's guarantee that what we think we want and need outside God's will can satisfy us. Don't believe it. You can never satisfy the desires of the flesh. Instead, "Blessed are they who hunger and thirst for righteousness, for they shall be satisfied" (Matthew 5:6). Only sustaining right relationships, living by the power of the Holy Spirit, and experiencing the fruit of the Spirit will satisfy you.[2]

Neil T. Anderson

---

3. How would you personally describe your struggle with the flesh? Write down your thoughts.

> I'm much more prone to sin than do good. Sin comes far more naturally to me and often leaves me wondering why I would ever want to do the things I do. The flesh is so enticing.

The word "flesh" reminds us that we are caught in the grip of sin. Even a desire for righteousness cannot enable us to actually become righteous. God deals with our flesh in a surprising way. He does not free us now from the fleshly nature. Instead, he provides a source of power that will release us from the domination of the flesh. Jesus has paid for sins generated by our flesh, whether sins of our past or those yet in our future. But Jesus has also provided us with his Holy Spirit. The Spirit lives within us, and he is the source of new desires and a new perspective.[3]

Lawrence O. Richards

Running with the Spirit

In answer to his question concerning who will set him free from his body of death, Paul exclaims, "Thanks be to God—through Jesus Christ our Lord!" (Romans 7:25) He continues in Romans 8 to explain that we have been delivered from the law of sin and death.

4. Read Romans 8:1-17, one of the richest passages in all of Scripture regarding laying aside the flesh and running with the Spirit.

   a. How have we been set free (verses 1-4)?

   Through Christ Jesus w/ the law of the Spirit.

   b. What are the evidences of the control of the old nature versus the control of the new nature (verses 5-8)?

   Having mind set on things the old nature desires.

   c. What gives us the ability to overcome the flesh (verses 9-11)?

   The Spirit of God

   d. What gives us the ability to run with the Spirit (verses 12-17)?

   Put to death the deeds of the flesh by the Spirit.

The Christian message of Christ's liberating act on the cross summons man from the only possible way of life open to him *kata sarka*, after the flesh, i.e. according to human standards and thinking. It calls him to live now *kata pneuma*, according to the Spirit. True freedom exists only where the Holy Spirit works in a man, becoming the principle of his life, and where man does not block his working.[4]

J. Blunck

Fixing Our Eyes on Jesus

5. The apostle John tells us that "the Word became flesh, and dwelt among us" (John 1:14, NASB). Meditate on Hebrews 2:14-18, and record your thoughts concerning how Jesus makes it possible for us to lay aside the old nature.

> Hold firmly to confidence ...?
> Jesus experienced the same temptations ~ He destroyed the devil (merciful high priest)

The purifying influence of the Spirit corrects the taste of the soul, whereby He savors those things that are holy and agreeable to God. Like one with discriminating taste, the Spirit chooses those things that are good and wholesome, and rejects those that are evil. And thus the Spirit of God leads and guides; He enables us to understand the commands and counsels of God's Word, and rightly to apply them.[5]

Jonathan Edwards

AUTHOR'S REFLECTION — William Gurnall writes, "The flesh is to you as the horse is to the rider — you cannot go on your journey without it."[6] I was encouraged — somewhat — to discover that laying aside the deeds of the flesh is a continual effort. As Gurnall says, we cannot go on our journey, or race, without it. We will always have to deal with the flesh until we finish the race.

I like the way J. B. Phillips translates part of the Corinthian passage: "I really fight!" To me this is the key. As I abide in Christ, I am given His Spirit to energize, guide, and strengthen me, but I am still responsible to choose not to yield to sin. Oswald Chambers states, "The first thing to do in examining the power that dominates me is to take hold of the unwelcome fact that I am responsible for being thus dominated."[7] Now that I am in Christ, I have the power and the ability to choose to live righteously, but it is my choice.

I have memorized Psalm 141:4 — "Do not incline my heart to any evil thing, to practice deeds of wickedness with men who do iniquity; and do not let me eat of their delicacies" (NASB). I am not particularly inclined to practice deeds of wickedness with evil men, but I am inclined to eat of their delicacies. It is helpful to me to memorize Scripture in fighting the flesh; in fact, we are told in Psalm 119:11 to hide God's Word in our hearts so that we will not sin. Abiding in Christ and His Word is necessary to running the race freely.

> Many Christians are unable to stand against the temptations of the world or of their old nature. They strive to do their best to fight against sin and to serve God, but they have no strength. They have never grasped the secret: The Lord Jesus will every day from heaven continue His work in them. But on one condition — the soul must give Him time each day to impart His love and His grace. Time alone with the Lord Jesus every day is the indispensable condition for growth and power.[8]
>
> *Andrew Murray*

YOUR REFLECTION—As you look back over this chapter, take time to record your thoughts concerning your struggle with sin and the flesh. Be specific in writing down any new observations or new goals in laying aside the flesh and running in the Spirit.

SUGGESTED SCRIPTURE MEMORY: 1 Corinthians 9:26-27

Laying Aside the World: *running* WITH GODLINESS

Never give your hearts to this world or to any of the things in it. A man cannot love the Father and love the world at the same time.

1 JOHN 2:15, PH

The greatest rebuke to the sin of our age is holy living.[1]

HERBERT LOCKYER

Satan is the prince of the world, but Christ came to deliver us from this domain of darkness into the Kingdom of light. We are told in Philippians 3:19 that our citizenship is now in heaven. One of the major hindrances we have to face in running our race is combating the incredible allure and pull of the world. Paul tells how Demas deserted him because he loved this present world (see 2 Timothy 4:10). Even though the world is full of enticements, God has equipped us to counter Satan's authority while we are here. We do have the power to lay aside the world and to live a godly life in our generation.

Laying Aside the World

1. If we are committed to finishing the race God has put before us, we must understand our relationship to the world. Scripture is very clear about how to associate with the age we live in. What do these verses tell us about how we are to respond to the world?

Luke 9:23-25

We must deny ourselves daily.
(So as not to forfeit our very self)

Romans 12:1-2

Do not conform to the world
live holy and pleasing to God

James 4:4

Friendship with the world
is hatred towards God.

1 John 2:15-17

If you love the world, the love
of the Father is not in you.

> Worldliness is not a matter of engaging in those practices that some question. It is unthinkingly adopting the perspectives, values, and attitudes of our culture, without bringing them under the judgment of God's Word. It is carrying on in our lives as if we did not know Jesus.[2]
>
> *Lawrence O. Richards*

2. According to the following passages, why is it dangerous to "love" the world?

    Ephesians 6:12

    We are Fighting against the Spiritual Forces of evil.

    1 Peter 5:8

    The devil is looking for someone to devour.

    1 John 5:19

    The world is under the control of the evil one.

---

3. The apostle John gives us this encouragement: "Greater is He who is in you than he who is in the world" (1 John 4:4, NASB). Since we are in the world, how do we overcome the Prince of this world? Write down your observations from the verses that follow.

    Ephesians 6:10-11

    Be strong in the Lord (armor of God)

    James 4:7-8

    Submit and come near to God and the devil will flee.

1 John 2:14

The word of God

1 John 5:4-5

Believe that Jesus is the Son of God.

---

4. What are the areas in which you tend to become entangled with the values and attitudes of worldly culture?

Fashion, entertainment, acquision of things, beauty, selfish ambition

---

5. What ways do you find effective for laying aside "the world" in your life?

Spending time w/ the Lord.

"Resist the devil, and he will flee from you." This is a promise and God will keep it. If we resist our adversary, God will compel him to flee and will give us the victory. . . . At the same time, we are not to stand on the adversary's ground anywhere by any attitude or disobedience, or we give him a terrible power over us, which, while God will restrain in great mercy and kindness, He will not fully remove until we get fully on holy ground. Therefore, we must be armed with the breastplate of righteousness, as well as the shield of faith, if we would successfully resist the prince of darkness and the principalities in heavenly places.[3]

A. B. Simpson

Running with Godliness

We are told in 1 Corinthians 2:12, "We have not received the spirit of the world but the Spirit who is from God, that we may understand what God has freely given us." Since we have the power of the Holy Spirit in our lives, we have the ability to make righteous choices and to pursue godliness. Godliness is choosing to please God in all that we do; it is exemplifying Jesus in our everyday lives.

6. The following passages reveal contrasting choices. In each case, write down what the choice was and why it was made.

Psalm 78:17-22

Israelites chose the food of the world because they loved the world.

Hebrews 11:24-26

Moses forsook the luxuries of Egypt because he viewed the things of the Lord as far more valuable.

The tests of the Christian life, though outwardly not so terrible, are even more likely to overcome us than those of the fiery age. We have to bear the sneer of the world — that is little. Its soft words, its oily speeches, and its hypocrisy are far worse. Our danger is that we grow rich and proud, give ourselves up to the fashions of this present evil world, and lose our faith. Or if wealth is not the trial, worldly care causes difficulty. . . . The devil little cares which it is, as long as he destroys our love for and confidence in Christ. We must be awake now, for we walk on dangerous ground. We are most likely to fall asleep to our undoing unless our faith in Jesus is a reality and our love for Him a fervent flame.[4]

Charles H. Spurgeon

---

7. What encouragement to pursue godliness can you find in the following passages?

1 Timothy 6:6-11

— We can take nothing out
of this world.

— The love of money is the root of
all kinds of evil.

Titus 2:11-14

We are waiting for the coming
of Christ.

8. One of the major ways we can begin to train ourselves to make godly choices is to think the truth. What insights do the following verses provide into the importance of our mindset in laying aside worldliness and running with godliness?

Romans 12:2

Only by having your mind renewed can you understand what God's will and what godliness is.

Colossians 3:1-4

Sight your minds on things above.

Romans 7:23 and 8:5-7 show that the center of all spiritual bondage is the mind. That's where the battle must be fought and won if you are to experience the freedom in Christ which is your inheritance. . . . Patterns of negative thinking and behavior are learned, and they can be unlearned through disciplined Bible study and counseling.[5]

Neil T. Anderson

Fixing Our Eyes on Jesus

In her beautiful hymn "Turn Your Eyes upon Jesus," Helen H. Lemmel penned the words, "Turn your eyes upon Jesus, look full in His wonderful face, and the things of earth will grow strangely dim in the light of His glory and grace." If Jesus Christ is the One we are running toward while we are on this earth, then we need to be reminded of His teachings concerning the world.

9. What does Jesus teach in the following verses about our life with Him in the world?

John 14:27

Jesus gives us his peace

John 15:18-19

The world should hate us because it also hated Jesus.

10. Based on what you know of Jesus' life and ministry, briefly describe an example of how you think He was "in" but not "of" the world.

He never sinned...

AUTHOR'S REFLECTION—It is so easy for me to want to accept the world's solution to my problems, stress, and pain: "buy, accumulate, indulge, vegetate, escape!" It is a continual battle to pursue godliness and to run the race with my eyes fixed on Jesus. Someone observed that the race we are in is really an obstacle course. How true! We may start out each day running fairly well but then the enemy begins to throw different kinds of barriers in our way.

It wouldn't be so bad if the obstacles were ugly and had warning signs saying, "This hindrance is dangerous to your spiritual health! Use your spiritual weapons! Overcome it!" Usually, though, the world's temptations offer instant relief or a pleasurable diversion. We easily get sidetracked and allow the world and the enemy to entangle us. I cannot love God and the world; I cannot run freely and swiftly if I'm clutching the things of this life.

I have found motivation to keep running the race in a thought from William Gurnall that there are no vacations in the Christian life. I cannot allow myself to "vacation" in the world. My rest, my encouragement, my joy must come from the Lord. His strength, as I sit at His feet and appropriate His Word each day, enables me to overcome Satan, the world, and the barriers ahead. Andrew Murray wrote, "Christian, you live in a dangerous world! Cleave fast to the Lord Jesus. But remember: There must be daily fellowship with Jesus. His love alone can expel the love of the world. Take time to be alone with your Lord."[6]

YOUR REFLECTION—As you review this lesson, meditate on the words of Galatians 6:14—"But may it never be that I would boast, except in the cross of our Lord Jesus Christ, through which the world has been crucified to me, and I to the world (NASB)." Write a prayer to God expressing how you would like to lay aside the world and run with godly freedom.

SUGGESTED SCRIPTURE MEMORY: 1 John 2:15

CHAPTER 11

LAYING ASIDE DISCOURAGEMENT: *running* WITH PERSEVERANCE

Consider him who endured such opposition from sinful men, so that you will not grow weary and lose heart.
HEBREWS 12:3

Still fight resolutely on, knowing that, in this spiritual combat, none is overcome but he who ceases to struggle and to trust in God.[1]
LORENZO SCUPOLI

Now that we have begun to understand our freedom in Christ, we must learn to lay aside discouragement as we run our race. We have much within us to oppose our freedom, and we have a powerful enemy who majors on discouraging those committed to loving and serving our Lord.

An important aspect of living our lives for the Lord is a steadfast determination to finish the race at all costs. The one who perseveres continues to run faithfully no matter what obstacles she encounters. "For though a righteous man falls seven times, he rises again" (Proverbs 24:16).

Discouragement may come into our lives, but with a steadfast heart we can confront despair, lay it aside, and continue the race.

Laying Aside Discouragement

1. Few writers surpass the psalmists in communicating the depths of their feelings. In the book of Psalms, hopelessness and dismay are honestly expressed and acknowledged.

    a. Read Psalm 77:1-15 and describe Asaph's discouragement with God.

    He felt as though God had forgotten about him because he wasn't receiving the help and encouragement he asked for.

    b. How did Asaph begin to work through his frustration (verses 11-15)? *— He reminded himself of who God was and all he had already done.*

2. a. In what ways are you especially susceptible to discouragement with God, or with running your race as a Christian?

    When my thoughts become overrun w/ doubts, and it feels like God is not there!

    b. How do you usually respond when you experience times of despondency?

There are moments in the life of all believers when God and his ways become unintelligible to them. They get lost in profound meditation, and nothing is left them but a desponding sigh. But we know from Paul the apostle that the Holy Spirit intercedes for believers with God, when they cannot utter their sighs (Romans 8:26).[2]

Augustus F. Tholuck

---

3. Paul certainly encountered many hindrances in his race. Yet he always seemed to be able to encourage others to trust God patiently and to continue the race. Read Romans 8:23-39 and record the truths found in these verses that teach us to overcome discouragement and persevere in the Christian life.

---

4. Which truths from the Scripture in question 3 are most helpful for you in laying aside discouragement?

Any time that we are tempted to doubt God's love for us, we should go back to the Cross. We should reason somewhat in this fashion: If God loved me enough to give His Son to die for me when I was His enemy, surely He loves me enough to care for me now that I am His child.

Having loved me to the ultimate extent at the Cross, He cannot possibly fail to love me in my times of adversity. Having given such a priceless gift as His Son, surely He will also give all else that is consistent with His glory and my good.[3]

Jerry Bridges

Running with Perseverance

5. Peter writes, "Dear friends, do not be surprised at the painful trial you are suffering, as though something strange were happening to you" (1 Peter 4:12). We are not to be surprised or discouraged at our trials. But Peter does offer help for standing firm in our adversity. What truths does he communicate in the following passages that will enable us to persevere?

1 Peter 1:3-9

1 Peter 5:8-11

6. What hope can you find in these passages for enduring hardship without being overwhelmed by discouragement?

> Resisting Satan means that we actively submit to God and come against Satan and all of his work against us, steadfast in the faith. This simply means a steady, consistent bringing of the great truths of the faith against Satan. It is not improper but very biblical to address yourself against Satan, resisting him with the doctrinal truth of our faith.[4]
>
> *Mark I. Bubeck*

7. No one persevered the way Paul did! Read the following passages, and then write a few sentences describing Paul's earnest desire to endure to the end.

1 Corinthians 9:24-27; 2 Corinthians 4:7-10; 2 Timothy 4:6-8

Perseverance does not mean "perfect." It means that we keep going. We do not quit when we find that we are not yet mature and that there is a long journey still before us . . . perseverance is not resignation, putting up with things the way they are, staying in the same old rut year after year after year, or being a doormat for people to wipe their feet on. Endurance is not a desperate hanging on but a traveling from strength to strength. . . . Perseverance is triumphant and alive.[5]

Eugene H. Peterson

Fixing Our Eyes on Jesus

8. Our eyes are to be fixed on Jesus, and only Him, as we run our race. Read Hebrews 12:1-3. How can this passage encourage you toward a steadfast determination to run faithfully no matter what obstacles you encounter?

May I run the race before me,
Strong and brave to face the foe,
Looking only unto Jesus
As I onward go.[6]

AUTHOR'S REFLECTION — When I am discouraged, I begin to pray. I tell the Lord my feelings and ask Him to help me understand why I'm depressed. The reasons vary — sin, tiredness, believing the enemy, not trusting God. I find that if I seek the truth about my circumstances, then it is the truth that can set me free to trust Him and to receive His grace and guidance in the midst of my adversity.

It is fixing my eyes on the One who is Truth that motivates me to overcome and keep running. I fix my eyes on Jesus by spending time in His presence — reading, studying, memorizing His Word, and praying to Him. It is the truth of the Word that frees. The psalmist said, "I will walk about in freedom, for I have sought out your precepts" (Psalm 119:45).

I can run the race with perseverance when my heart's desire is to do His will and to trust Him with my life. His Spirit, then, guides, empowers, disciplines, and protects me. My race is run in freedom because the race becomes the Lord's, not mine.

I want to persevere in my race because I want to finish well. I don't want to limp across into heaven and be a workman who is ashamed when I see the Lord. There was a race in ancient Greece in which the runners had to finish with their torches burning. That's what I want — to finish with my torch burning. I want to be able to say what Paul said: "I have fought the good fight, I have finished the race, I have kept the faith" (2 Timothy 4:7). The only way I can continue to fight, finish the race, and keep the faith is to lay aside every encumbrance, and the sin which so easily entangles, and run with endurance the race that is set before me, fixing my eyes on Jesus. If my heart is set to live life in this way, then I will become a woman of freedom.

YOUR REFLECTION—Reflect on where you are in the process of experiencing God's freedom. Write down the burdens you most want to lay aside at this time in your life. Then write out, perhaps in the form of a prayer to the Lord, your desire to persevere in the race that God has called you to as His woman of freedom.

SUGGESTED SCRIPTURE MEMORY: Hebrews 12:3

NOTES

Chapter One — Laying Aside Hindrances:
Running with Freedom

1. J. Blunck, in *The New International Dictionary of New Testament Theology*, vol. 1, edited by Colin Brown (Grand Rapids, MI: Zondervan, 1971), 718.

2. Matthew Henry, *Matthew Henry's Commentary,* vol. 5 (Iowa Falls, IA: Riverside Book & Bible House, n.d.), 995.

3. Hannah Whitall Smith, *The Christian's Secret of a Happy Life* (Westwood, NJ: Fleming H. Revell, n.d.), 38.

4. G. Campbell Morgan, quoted in *Closer Walk* (Walk Thru the Bible Ministries, Inc.), 27 August 1989.

5. Henry, 953.

6. Nancy Groom, *From Bondage to Bonding: Escaping Codependency, Embracing Biblical Love* (Colorado Springs, CO: NavPress, 1991), 117.

7. Lawrence O. Richards, *Expository Dictionary of Bible Words* (Grand Rapids, MI: Zondervan, 1985), 296.

8. Whitall Smith, 38.

Chapter Two — Laying Aside the Old Self:
Running with the New Self

1. Teresa of Avila, quoted in *The New Book of Christian Quotations,* compiled by Tony Castle (New York: Crossroad, 1989), 220.

2. George MacDonald, quoted in *Trusting God,* by Jerry Bridges (Colorado Springs, CO: NavPress, 1988), 162-163.

3. Neil T. Anderson, *The Bondage Breaker* (Eugene, OR: Harvest House, 1990), 141.

4. Hannah Whitall Smith, quoted in *Joy and Strength,* edited by Mary Wilder Tileston (Minneapolis, MN: World Wide, 1988), 242.

5. Henrietta Mears, *Closer Walk* (Walk Thru the Bible Ministries, Inc.), 24 April 1991.

Chapter Three — Laying Aside the Past:
Running with an Eternal Perspective

1. A. W. Tozer, *The Root of the Righteous* (Harrisburg, PA: Christian Publications, 1955), 62.

2. Nancy Groom, *From Bondage to Bonding: Escaping Codependency, Embracing Biblical Love* (Colorado Springs, CO: NavPress, 1991), 166.

3. Charles H. Spurgeon, quoted in *Closer Walk* (Walk Thru the Bible Ministries, Inc.), 13 February 1990.

4. Oswald Chambers, *My Utmost for His Highest* (Westwood, NJ: Barbour and Company, 1935), 31 December.

5. Amy Carmichael, *Thou Givest . . . They Gather* (Fort Washington, PA: Christian Literature Crusade, 1958), 186.

6. Groom, 179.

7. Dan Allender, *The Wounded Heart: Hope for Adult Victims of Childhood Sexual Abuse* (Colorado Springs, CO: NavPress, 1990), 247.

Chapter Four — Laying Aside Pleasing People:
Running with Fellowship

1. Dan Allender, *The Wounded Heart: Hope for Adult Victims of Childhood Sexual Abuse* (Colorado Springs, CO: NavPress, 1990), 174.

2. Nancy Groom, *From Bondage to Bonding: Escaping Codependency, Embracing Biblical Love* (Colorado Springs, CO: NavPress, 1991), 35.

3. Groom, 35.

4. Lawrence O. Richards, *Expository Dictionary of Bible Words* (Grand Rapids, MI: Zondervan, 1985), 276.

5. Matthew Henry, *Matthew Henry's Commentary*, vol. 6 (Iowa Falls, IA: Riverside Book & Bible House, n.d.), 482-483.

6. Oswald Chambers, *My Utmost for His Highest* (Westwood, NJ: Barbour and Company, 1935), 31 May.

Chapter Five — Laying Aside Bitterness:
Running with Forgiveness

1. Hugh Black, quoted in *Joy and Strength*, edited by Mary Wilder Tileston (Minneapolis, MN: World Wide, 1988), 245.

2. W. E. Vine, *An Expository Dictionary of New Testament Words* (Old Tappan, NJ: Fleming H. Revell, 1966), 55.

3. Vine, 129.

4. J. I. Rodale, *The Synonym Finder* (Emmaus, PA: Warner Books Edition, 1978), 116-117.

5. Lawrence O. Richards, *Expository Dictionary of Bible Words* (Grand Rapids, MI: Zondervan, 1985), 127-128.

6. Jerry Bridges, *The Pursuit of Holiness* (Colorado Springs, CO: NavPress, 1978), 122.

7. Oswald Chambers, *My Utmost for His Highest* (Westwood, NJ: Barbour and Company, 1935), 20 November.

8. Neil T. Anderson, *The Bondage Breaker* (Eugene, OR: Harvest House, 1990), 195, 197.

9. Charles Swindoll, *Growing Strong in the Seasons of Life* (Portland, OR: Multnomah, 1983), 167.

10. Chambers, 26 June.

Chapter Six — Laying Aside Busyness: *Running with Rest*

1. Lawrence O. Richards, *Expository Dictionary of Bible Words* (Grand Rapids, MI: Zondervan, 1985), 524.

2. Charles Swindoll, *Growing Strong in the Seasons of Life* (Portland, OR: Multnomah, 1983), 175-176.

3. John Kenneth Mackenzie, quoted in *Joy and Strength*, edited by Mary Wilder Tileston (Minneapolis, MN: World Wide, 1988), 49.

4. Charles Hummel, "The Tyranny of the Urgent," in *Discipleship Journal* 10, no. 6 (Issue Sixty, November/December 1990), 27.

5. Oswald Chambers, *My Utmost for His Highest* (Westwood, NJ: Barbour and Company, 1935), 11 June.

6. James D. Burns, quoted in *The Treasury of David*, by Charles H. Spurgeon, vol. 1 (McLean, VA: MacDonald, n.d.), 184.

7. W. H. Griffith Thomas, quoted in *Closer Walk* (Walk Thru the Bible Ministries, Inc.), June 1990.

8. Frank Barker with Maureen Rank, "The Martha Syndrome," *Discipleship Journal* 8, no. 2 (Issue Forty-four, March 1988), 12.

9. Chambers, 4 August.

Chapter Seven — Laying Aside Anxiety:
Running with Peace

1. Lawrence O. Richards, *Expository Dictionary of Bible Words* (Grand Rapids, MI: Zondervan, 1985), 58.

2. J. I. Rodale, *The Synonym Finder* (Emmaus, PA: Warner Books Edition, 1978), 55.

3. Oswald Chambers, *My Utmost for His Highest* (Westwood, NJ: Barbour and Company, 1935), 4 July.

4. Richards, 58.

5. Jerry Bridges, *Transforming Grace: Living Confidently in God's Unfailing Love* (Colorado Springs, CO: NavPress, 1991), 186.

6. Robert Jamieson, A. R. Fausset, and David Brown, *Commentary on the Whole Bible*, rev. ed. (Grand Rapids, MI: Zondervan, 1961), 1311.

7. Charles H. Spurgeon, *The Treasury of David*, vol. 2 (McLean, VA: MacDonald, n.d.), 147.

8. A. B. Simpson, quoted in *Closer Walk* (Walk Thru the Bible Ministries, Inc.), 24/25 August, 1991.

Chapter Eight — Laying Aside Doubt and Fear:
Running with Faith and Trust

1. Jerry Bridges, *Trusting God* (Colorado Springs, CO: NavPress, 1988), 155.

2. Dan Allender, *The Wounded Heart: Hope for Adult Victims of Childhood Sexual Abuse* (Colorado Springs, CO: NavPress, 1990), 176.

3. Oswald Chambers, *My Utmost for His Highest* (Westwood, NJ: Barbour and Company, 1935), 3 December.

4. Eugene H. Peterson, *A Long Obedience in the Same Direction* (Downers Grove, IL: InterVarsity, 1980), 122-124.

5. William Gurnall, *The Christian in Complete Armour*, rev. and abridged, vol. 1 (Carlisle, PA: Banner of Truth Trust, 1986), 112-113.

Chapter Nine — Laying Aside the Flesh:
Running with the Spirit

1. Charles H. Spurgeon, quoted in *Closer Walk* (Walk Thru the Bible Ministries, Inc.), 2 September 1991.

2. Neil T. Anderson, *The Bondage Breaker* (Eugene, OR: Harvest House, 1990), 135.

3. Lawrence O. Richards, *Expository Dictionary of Bible Words* (Grand Rapids, MI: Zondervan, 1985), 285.

4. J. Blunck, in *The New International Dictionary of New Testament Theology*, vol. 1, edited by Colin Brown (Grand Rapids, MI: Zondervan, 1971), 719.

5. Jonathan Edwards, quoted in *Closer Walk* (Walk Thru the Bible Ministries, Inc.), 19 March 1991.

6. William Gurnall, *The Christian in Complete Armour*, rev. and abridged, vol. 1 (Carlisle, PA: Banner of Truth Trust, 1986), 127.

7. Oswald Chambers, *My Utmost for His Highest* (Westwood, NJ: Barbour and Company, 1935), 14 March.

8. Andrew Murray, quoted in *Closer Walk* (Walk Thru the Bible Ministries, Inc.), 21/22 April 1990.

Chapter Ten — Laying Aside the World:
Running with Godliness

1. Herbert Lockyer, "Getting Ready for the End," *Decision Magazine* (March 1985).

2. Lawrence O. Richards, *Expository Dictionary of Bible Words* (Grand Rapids, MI: Zondervan, 1985), 639.

3. A. B. Simpson, quoted in *Closer Walk* (Walk Thru the Bible Ministries, Inc.), 29/30 July 1989.

4. Charles H. Spurgeon, quoted in *Closer Walk* (Walk Thru the Bible Ministries, Inc.), 21 September 1990.

5. Neil T. Anderson, *The Bondage Breaker* (Eugene, OR: Harvest House, 1990), 52-53.

6. Andrew Murray, quoted in *Closer Walk* (Walk Thru the Bible Ministries, Inc.), 20 August 1991.

Chapter Eleven — Laying Aside Discouragement:
Running with Perseverance

1. Lorenzo Scupoli, quoted in *Joy and Strength*, edited by Mary Wilder Tileston (Minneapolis, MN: World Wide, 1988), 228.

2. Augustus F. Tholuck, quoted in *The Treasury of David*, by Charles H. Spurgeon, vol. 2 (McLean, VA: MacDonald, n.d.), 319.

3. Jerry Bridges, *Trusting God* (Colorado Springs, CO: NavPress, 1988), 140.

4. Mark I. Bubeck, *The Adversary* (Chicago, IL: Moody, 1975), 100.

5. Eugene H. Peterson, *A Long Obedience in the Same Direction* (Downers Grove, IL: InterVarsity, 1980), 127.

6. From the hymn "May the Mind of Christ, My Savior," lyrics by Kate B. Wilkinson.

AUTHOR

*C*ynthia Hall Heald is a native Texan. She and her husband, Jack, a veterinarian by profession, are on full-time staff with The Navigators in Tucson, Arizona. They have four children: Melinda, Daryl, Shelly, and Michael.

Cynthia graduated from the University of Texas with a BA in English. She speaks frequently to church women's groups and at seminars and retreats.

Cynthia is also the author of the NavPress Bible studies *Becoming a Woman of Excellence, Becoming a Woman of Purpose, Becoming a Woman of Prayer, Intimacy with God,* and *Loving Your Husband* (companion study to *Loving Your Wife* by Jack and Cynthia), and *Becoming a Woman Who Walks with God.*

Become a Woman of God

 ### Becoming a Woman of Purpose
If your goals and success leave you feeling unsatisfied, use this study to gain a better understanding of God's purpose for your life—to love and serve Him.

Cynthia Heald   978-1-57683-831-0

 ### Becoming a Woman of Prayer
God designed women to seek Him in all they do. This Bible study will encourage you to become a woman whose life is characterized by constant conversation with God.

Cynthia Heald   978-1-57683-830-3

 ### Becoming a Woman of Excellence
This best-selling Bible study has helped over one million women understand who God designed them to be. Discover the freedom you have to serve and please God.

Cynthia Heald   978-1-57683-832-7

> "Deep in my heart is the constant prayer that I would be a woman who consistently walks with God."
> —Cynthia Heald—

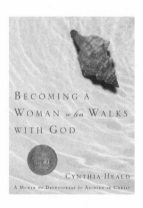

Becoming a Woman Who Walks with God
978-1-57683-733-7

Essential to walking with God is maintaining communion with Him. This devotional book, designed to guide you through a month of quiet times, emphasizes the joy and the importance of abiding in Christ.

Each of the thirty-one daily meditations in this collection includes a Scripture passage, insights from the author, a thought-provoking quote from a classic Christian writer or thinker, a question to ponder during the day, and a short topical prayer.

Join Cynthia on a journey of reflection and worship, and discover the joy of becoming a woman who walks with God.

MAYBE GOD IS RIGHT AFTER ALL

AND OTHER RADICAL IDEAS TO LIVE BY

CYNTHIA HEALD

Best-selling author of *Becoming a Woman of Excellence*

In *Maybe God Is Right After All,* Cynthia Heald
offers ten bottom-line truths, tested and proven in her
own journey, to equip readers to make godly choices
at the crossroads of their own life circumstances.

Softcover
ISBN 1-4143-0084-0

Release date:
OCTOBER 2005

TYNDALE